The 5-Day Rapid Weight Loss Plan

Easy and Effective Strategies for Losing Weight at Home

Katherine Martin

Copyright © Katherine Martin 2023

All Rights Reserved

Table of contents

Introduction

Chapter One

The Importance of a Rapid Weight Loss Plan

Chapter Two

Understanding Your Body and Weight Loss

Chapter Three

Meal Planning for Rapid Weight Loss

Chapter Four

Quick and Easy Home Workouts

Chapter Five

Making Healthy Food Choices

Chapter Six

Mindfulness and Meditation for Weight Loss

Chapter Seven

Overcoming Emotional Eating and Other Obstacles

Chapter Eight

Staying on Track and Maintaining Your Results

Chapter Nine

Putting it all Together: The 5-Day Rapid Weight Loss Plan

Chapter Conclusion

Achieving Your Weight Loss Goals and Living a Healthier Life

Introduction

"Are you tired of feeling frustrated and defeated by your weight loss journey? Are you ready to finally achieve the results you've been dreaming of? Look no further. The 5-Day Rapid Weight Loss Plan is here to help you lose weight quickly and easily in the comfort of your own home.

This book is designed for anyone who wants to lose weight but feels like they don't have the time, energy, or resources to do it. In this book, you will learn effective and easy strategies for weight loss that you can start implementing right away. From simple meal plans to quick and easy home workout routines, this book provides everything you need to know to jumpstart your weight loss journey and achieve your goals.

With The 5-Day Rapid Weight Loss Plan, you'll learn how to lose weight fast and maintain your results for the long term, so you can finally feel confident and proud of your body. Get ready to say goodbye to feeling stuck and hello to a new, healthier, and happier you!"

"In this book, you'll discover how to:
Kickstart your metabolism with a 5-day rapid weight loss plan
Create easy and delicious meal plans that will keep you on track
Incorporate simple home workouts that will help you burn calories and tone your body
Learn to make healthy food choices that will support your weight loss goals
Discover the power of mindfulness and meditation in weight loss

Learn how to overcome emotional eating and other common obstacles that can sabotage your weight loss efforts

The 5-Day Rapid Weight Loss Plan is not just about losing weight, it's about transforming your life. It's about learning how to make healthy choices and developing habits that will support your weight loss goals for the long term. With this book, you will have all the tools and knowledge you need to start your weight loss journey and achieve the results you want.

So, what are you waiting for? Don't let another day go by feeling frustrated and defeated by your weight loss efforts. Take control of your health and start your weight loss journey today with The 5-Day Rapid Weight Loss Plan."

Chapter One

The Importance of a Rapid Weight Loss Plan

This introduction will provide an overview of the importance of a rapid weight loss plan and what readers can expect to learn from the book.

Overview

This section will provide an overview of the book and the purpose of the 5-day rapid weight loss plan. It will explain how the plan is designed to help individuals kickstart their weight loss journey and achieve rapid results.

Benefits of a rapid weight loss plan

This section will discuss the benefits of a rapid weight loss plan. It will explain how a rapid weight loss plan can help individuals achieve weight loss results quickly, boost motivation, and jumpstart long-term weight loss efforts.

What you will learn

This section will provide a preview of the key concepts and strategies that will be covered in the book. It will include topics such as meal planning, home workouts, mindfulness and meditation, and strategies for overcoming obstacles.

Who this book is for

This section will explain who the book is intended for and what readers can expect to gain from it. It will highlight that the book is suitable for anyone looking to lose weight quickly and easily at home, regardless of their fitness level or prior experience.

Conclusion

In conclusion, this introduction will provide an overview of the importance of a rapid weight loss plan and what readers can expect to learn from the book. It will provide a clear understanding of the benefits of a rapid weight loss plan and the key concepts and strategies that will be covered in the book.

Chapter Two

Understanding Your Body and Weight Loss

This chapter aims to provide a comprehensive understanding of the human body and its relation to weight loss. It will cover key concepts such as metabolism, calorie intake and expenditure, and the role of hormones in weight loss.

1.1 Metabolism 101

In this section, we will explore the basics of metabolism and how it affects weight loss. It is the rate at which the body burns calories and is determined by factors such as age, sex, genetics, and muscle mass. A faster metabolism means that the body burns calories more quickly, which can make weight loss easier.

1.2 Calorie intake and expenditure

This section will cover the importance of balancing calorie intake and expenditure to achieve weight loss. The body needs a certain number of calories to function properly, but if you consume more calories than you burn, the excess will be stored as fat. To lose weight, it is important to create a calorie deficit, which can be achieved by reducing calorie intake, increasing physical activity, or a combination of both.

1.3 Hormones and weight loss

In this section, we will examine the role of hormones in weight loss. Hormones such as insulin, cortisol, and thyroid hormones play a significant role in regulating metabolism and appetite. Understanding how these hormones affect weight loss can help you make better choices in terms of diet and exercise.

1.4 Setting realistic weight loss goals

This section will cover the importance of setting realistic weight loss goals. Crash diets and unrealistic weight loss goals can be dangerous and lead to yo-yo dieting. Instead, it's important to set goals that are achievable and sustainable in the long term. This section will guide how to set realistic weight loss goals and how to measure progress.

1.5 Conclusion

In conclusion, understanding your body and weight loss is essential for achieving your weight loss goals. By understanding the basics of metabolism, calorie intake and expenditure, and the role of hormones, you can make informed decisions about your diet and exercise plan. Setting realistic weight loss goals and tracking progress will help you stay motivated and on track.

Chapter Three

Meal Planning for Rapid Weight Loss

This chapter will focus on the importance of meal planning in achieving rapid weight loss. It will cover key concepts such as nutrient-dense foods, portion control, and meal prep strategies.

2.1 Nutrient-dense foods

In this section, we will discuss the importance of consuming nutrient-dense foods for weight loss. By incorporating nutrient-dense foods into your diet, you can feel full and satisfied while still creating a calorie deficit.

2.2 Portion control

This section will cover the importance of portion control in weight loss. Consuming too many calories, even from healthy foods, can impede weight loss. By learning how to control portion sizes, you can achieve weight loss while still enjoying a variety of foods.

2.3 Meal prep strategies

This section will guide how to make meal planning and preparation easy and efficient. Meal prep strategies such as prepping ingredients in advance, cooking in bulk, and using a meal planning template can help save time and keep you on track.

2.4 Meal planning for different dietary needs

This section will cover how to tailor meal planning to different dietary needs such as vegetarian, vegan, gluten-free, and low-carb diets. It will provide tips on how to make substitutions and adapt recipes to suit different dietary needs.

2.5 Conclusion

Meal planning is an essential part of achieving rapid weight loss. By consuming nutrient-dense foods, practicing portion control, and utilizing meal prep strategies, you can create a calorie deficit and achieve your weight loss goals. Meal planning for different dietary needs can also make it easier to stick to your diet.

Chapter Four

Quick and Easy Home Workouts

This chapter will focus on the importance of regular physical activity in achieving rapid weight loss and guide how to create an effective home workout routine.

3.1 The benefits of physical activity

In this section, we will discuss the many benefits of regular physical activity for weight loss.

3.2 Creating a home workout routine

This section will guide how to create an effective home workout routine. It will cover different types of exercises such as cardio, strength training, and HIIT, and how to design a workout plan that is tailored to your fitness level and goals. It will also provide tips on how to make use of minimal equipment or even no equipment at all.

3.3 Incorporating variety

This section will cover the importance of incorporating variety into your home workout routine. By switching up your exercises and keeping your workout challenging, you can prevent boredom and plateaus, and continue to see results.

3.4 Scheduling and consistency

This section will discuss the importance of consistency in a home workout routine. It will provide tips on how to schedule your workouts to make them a regular part of your routine, and how to stay motivated to keep up with your workout routine.

3.5 Conclusion

Regular physical activity is an essential part of achieving rapid weight loss. By creating an effective home workout routine, you can burn calories, increase muscle mass, and improve your overall health and well-being. Incorporating variety and consistency in your routine can help you see results faster and make it easier to stick to your workout plan.

Chapter Five

Making Healthy Food Choices

This chapter will focus on how to make healthy food choices that support weight loss. It will cover key concepts such as nutrient-dense foods, mindful eating, and how to make better food choices when eating out.

4.1 Nutrient-dense foods

In this section, we will discuss the importance of consuming nutrient-dense foods for weight loss.4.1 Rich in nutrients meals

We will cover the significance of eating nutrient-dense foods for weight reduction in this part. Foods that are abundant in nutrients yet low in calories are said to be nutrient-dense. These include fresh produce, whole grains, lean proteins, lean proteins, and healthy fats. You may feel full and satisfied while maintaining a calorie deficit by including nutrient-dense items in your diet. By incorporating nutrient-dense foods into your diet, you can feel full.

4.2 Mindful eating

This section will cover the importance of mindful eating in weight loss. Mindful eating involves paying attention to your body's hunger and fullness cues and eating in response to those cues rather than emotions or external triggers. By practicing mindful eating, you can make better food choices and avoid overeating.

4.3 Making better food choices when eating out

This section will guide how to make healthier food choices when eating out. It will cover how to navigate restaurant menus, how to make modifications to dishes, and how to order in a way that supports weight loss.

4.4 Reading food labels

This section will cover the importance of understanding food labels and how to use them to make better food choices. It will cover how to read and interpret ingredient lists, nutrition facts, and other information on food labels.

4.5 Conclusion

Making healthy food choices is an essential part of achieving weight loss. By consuming nutrient-dense foods, practicing mindful eating, and making better food choices when eating out, you can create a calorie deficit and achieve your weight loss goals. Understanding food labels can also help you make better food choices and support your weight loss efforts.

Chapter Six

Mindfulness and Meditation for Weight Loss

This chapter will focus on the power of mindfulness and meditation in weight loss. It will cover key concepts such as mindfulness practices, meditation techniques, and how to incorporate mindfulness and meditation into a weight loss routine.

5.1 Mindfulness practices

In this section, we will discuss the benefits of mindfulness practices for weight loss. Mindfulness practices such as mindful eating, body scanning, and mindful movement can help you become more aware of your body's hunger and fullness cues, reduce stress and improve overall well-being.

5.2 Meditation techniques

This section will cover different meditation techniques and how they can support weight loss. Techniques such as guided imagery, visualization, and loving-kindness meditation can help reduce stress, improve self-awareness, and increase feelings of self-compassion.

5.3 Incorporating mindfulness and meditation into a weight loss routine

This section will guide how to incorporate mindfulness and meditation practices into a weight loss routine. It will cover how to create a mindfulness and meditation practice that is tailored to your needs, schedule, and goals.

5.4 Overcoming obstacles

This section will discuss common obstacles that can arise when incorporating mindfulness and meditation practices into a weight loss routine and provide strategies for overcoming them.

5.5 Conclusion

Mindfulness and meditation practices can be powerful tools for weight loss. By becoming more aware of your body's hunger and fullness cues, reducing stress, and improving overall well-being, you can make better food choices and stay motivated to achieve your weight loss goals. Incorporating mindfulness and meditation practices into your weight loss routine can also help you overcome obstacles and stay on track.

Chapter Seven

Overcoming Emotional Eating and Other Obstacles

This chapter will focus on common obstacles that can impede weight loss, specifically emotional eating, and provide strategies for overcoming them. It will cover key concepts such as identifying triggers, developing coping mechanisms, and building resilience.

6.1 Understanding emotional eating

In this section, we will discuss the concept of emotional eating and how it can contribute to weight gain. Emotional eating refers to the tendency to eat in response to emotions rather than hunger. By identifying the emotional triggers that lead to emotional eating, individuals can learn to manage their emotions more healthily and make better food choices.

6.2 Identifying triggers

This section will guide how to identify the triggers that lead to emotional eating. It will cover techniques such as journaling, mindfulness practices, and self-reflection to help individuals become more aware of their emotions and triggers.

6.3 Developing coping mechanisms

This section will cover different coping mechanisms that can be used to manage emotions and reduce emotional eating. Coping mechanisms such as mindfulness practices, exercise, and talking to a therapist can help individuals develop healthier ways to manage their emotions.

6.4 Building resilience

This section will cover the importance of building resilience in overcoming obstacles to weight loss. Resilience is the ability to cope with adversity and bounce back from setbacks. It will provide strategies for building resilience such as setting realistic goals, developing a support system, and practicing self-compassion.

6.5 Conclusion

Emotional eating is a common obstacle that can impede weight loss. By understanding emotional eating, identifying triggers, developing coping mechanisms, and building resilience, individuals can learn to manage their emotions more healthily and achieve their weight loss goals. It's important to understand that overcoming obstacles to weight loss is not a one-time event, but a continuous journey that requires ongoing effort and support.

Chapter Eight

Staying on Track and Maintaining Your Results

This chapter will focus on strategies for staying on track with weight loss goals and maintaining results over the long term. It will cover key concepts such as goal setting, tracking progress, creating accountability, and developing a sustainable plan.

7.1 Setting and tracking goals

In this section, we will discuss the importance of setting and tracking goals for weight loss. Setting specific, measurable, and realistic goals is crucial for achieving weight loss results. Additionally, tracking progress can help individuals stay motivated and on track with their goals.

7.2 Creating accountability

This section will cover the importance of creating accountability in weight loss. Creating accountability can be done through working with a coach, joining a support group, or enlisting a friend or family member as a weight loss partner. Having an accountability partner can help keep individuals motivated and on track.

7.3 Developing a sustainable plan

This section will guide how to create a sustainable weight loss plan. It will cover how to create a balanced and realistic plan that can be sustained over the long term. This can include things such as incorporating physical activity into daily routine, making healthy food choices, and developing mindfulness and meditation practices.

7.4 Overcoming obstacles

This section will discuss common obstacles that can arise when trying to maintain weight loss results and provide strategies for overcoming them. These can include things such as overcoming plateaus, dealing with setbacks, and staying motivated.

7.5 Conclusion

Staying on track and maintaining weight loss results is a continuous journey that requires ongoing effort and support. By setting and tracking goals, creating accountability, developing a sustainable plan, and overcoming obstacles, individuals can achieve their weight loss goals and maintain their results over the long term.

Chapter Nine

Putting it all Together: The 5-Day Rapid Weight Loss Plan

This chapter will provide a detailed and actionable plan for achieving rapid weight loss within 5 days. It will cover key concepts such as meal planning, home workouts, mindfulness and meditation practices, and strategies for staying on track.

8.1 The 5-Day Rapid Weight Loss Plan

In this section, we will provide a comprehensive plan for achieving weight loss within 5 days. The plan will include detailed meal plans, home workout routines, mindfulness and meditation practices, and strategies for staying on track.

8.2 Meal planning

This section will guide how to create a meal plan that supports weight loss. It will include nutrient-dense food options, portion control, and meal prep strategies.

8.3 Home workout routines

This section will provide home workout routines that are designed to burn calories and tone the body. The routines will include a variety of exercises such as cardio, strength training, and HIIT.

8.4 Mindfulness and meditation practices

This section will guide how to incorporate mindfulness and meditation practices into the 5-day rapid weight loss plan. It will include practices such as mindful eating, body scanning, and visualization

Chapter Conclusion

Achieving Your Weight Loss Goals and Living a Healthier Life

This conclusion will summarize the key concepts and strategies discussed in the book and provide readers with guidance on how to continue their weight loss journey.

Recap of key concepts

This section will provide a summary of the key concepts and strategies discussed throughout the book. It will include topics such as nutrient-dense foods, home workouts, mindfulness and meditation, and strategies for overcoming obstacles.

Continued weight loss journey

This section will guide how to continue the weight loss journey after the 5-day plan has been completed. It will include strategies for maintaining weight loss results, setting long-term goals, and creating a sustainable weight loss plan.

Importance of self-care

This section will emphasize the importance of self-care in the weight loss journey. It will guide how to incorporate self-care practices such as sleep, stress management, and relaxation into the daily routine to support weight loss and overall well-being.

Final thoughts

This section will provide final thoughts and encouraging words for readers who are on their weight loss journey. It will remind readers that weight loss is a process and that progress may not be linear. The section will encourage readers to be kind to themselves and celebrate small successes along the way.

Conclusion

In conclusion, this chapter will summarize the key concepts and strategies discussed in the book and provide readers with guidance on how to continue their weight loss journey. It will also emphasize the importance.

www.ingramcontent.com/pod-product-compliance
Lightning Source LLC
Chambersburg PA
CBHW050323220526
45465CB00005B/2109